The
Cuban Missile Crisis:
A World in Peril

Edited by Karl E. Valois

View of San Cristobal, showing extensive vehicle tracks, indicating increased activity from previous photos, 10/23/62 (U.S. Dept. of Defense)

Discovery Enterprises, Ltd.
Carlisle, Massachusetts

© Discovery Enterprises, Ltd., Carlisle, MA 1998

ISBN 1-878668-92-7 paperback edition
Library of Congress Catalog Card Number 97-78308

10 9 8 7 6 5 4 3 2 1

Printed in the United States of America

Subject Reference Guide:

The Cuban Missile Crisis: A World in Peril
edited by Karl E. Valois

Cuban Missile Crisis — U. S. History

President John F. Kennedy — U. S. History

Soviet-American Relations — U. S. History

Photo Credits:

Cover graphic: Target coverage of Soviet missiles based in Cuba, courtesy of the John F. Kennedy Library.

Photos and documents from the National Archives, except where other credits for photos appear in text.

Editor's notes regarding the documents:

1. *All original spelling has been retained.*

2. *A full line of dots indicates the deletion of at least an entire paragraph.*

Table of Contents

Dedication

Alyssa, Ryan, Nathan, Jared
and my parents,
Jack and Heidi Valois

"All the News That's Fit to Print"

The New York Times.

LATE CITY EDITION

VOL. CXII...No. 38,256.

NEW YORK, TUESDAY, OCTOBER 23, 1962.

FIVE CENTS

U.S. IMPOSES ARMS BLOCKADE ON CUBA ON FINDING OFFENSIVE-MISSILE SITES; KENNEDY READY FOR SOVIET SHOWDOWN

U.S. JUDGES GIVEN POWER TO REQUIRE VOTE FOR NEGROES

High Court Upholds Order Forcing the Registration of 54 in Alabama County

Chinese Open New Front; Use Tanks Against Indians

Nehru Warns of Peril to Independence —Reds Attack Near Burmese Border and Press Two Other Drives

SHIPS MUST STOP

Other Action Planned If Big Rockets Are Not Dismantled

By JAMES RESTON

ANNOUNCES HIS ACTION: President Kennedy speaking to the nation last night on radio and television. He told of moves to keep offensive equipment away from Cuba.

PRESIDENT GRAVE

Asserts Russians Lied and Put Hemisphere in Great Danger

By ANTHONY LEWIS

U.S. Bids U.N. Bar China; Denounces Attack on India

By SAM POPE BREWER

U.S. SAID TO EASE KATANGA POLICY

Reported Willing to Put Off Any Economic Sanctions —Congolese Disturbed

By LLOYD GARRISON

TRAFFIC DELAYED AT BERLIN BORDER

Reds Start Intensive Check of Civilian Trucks an Hour Before Kennedy Speech

By SYDNEY GRUSON

Moscow Says U.S. Holds 'Armed Fist' Over Cuba

By SEYMOUR TOPPING

BIG FORCE MASSES TO BLOCKADE CUBA

Armada Is Under Orders to Open Fire if Necessary— All Troops Are Alerted

By JACK RAYMOND

Navy Ready to Act

102 SAVED AT SEA AS PLANE DITCHES

Rescue in Wake of Alaska Minutes After Accident

Canada Asks Inspection of Cuba; Britain Supporting Quarantine

Diefenbaker Comments
By RAYMOND DANIELL

British Note Peril
By DREW MIDDLETON

All Military Forces Mobilized by Castro

KENNEDY CANCELS CAMPAIGN TALKS

He and Johnson Take Steps to Concentrate on Crisis

By CABELL PHILLIPS

Stocks Plunge Early On Crisis, but Rally

By RICHARD RUTTER

Front page of The New York Times, *October 23, 1962*

Introduction

by
Karl E. Valois

In the half century since the dawning of the atomic age in 1945, no event has more seriously imperiled the continued existence of civilization, as we know it, than the Cuban missile crisis. For thirteen terrifying days in October, 1962, leaders in the United States and the Soviet Union held top-secret meetings, made military preparations, and issued horrifying threats over the placement of Russian atomic weapons in Cuba. Only after the two superpowers had brought the world to the very brink of a nuclear Armageddon did reason and wisdom prevail.

The seeds of the controversy were sown in the stormy history of American-Cuban relations. Despite the resentment of many on the Caribbean island, the United States for decades had secured a strong political and economic foothold. By the late 1950s, American businessmen, with the support of Cuban president Fulgencio Batista, were in firm control of sugar, mining, and public utilities enterprises and had investments totalling $1 billion. Rallying behind the anti-Yankee nationalism of Fidel Castro, however, rebel forces overthrew the corrupt and dictatorial Batista in 1959.

Once in power, Castro launched economic, political, and social policies calculated to end U.S. domination. He began to nationalize American companies, brutally executed Batista's supporters, cancelled elections, and sounded the call for the spread of similar revolutions throughout Latin America. After Cuba completed a trade agreement with the U.S.S.R., President Dwight D. Eisenhower, in March of 1960, directed the C.I.A. to prepare a covert operation for the Cuban leader's removal from power. In addition, the U.S. cut off all purchases of Cuban sugar and ended all exports to the island. As a result, Castro quickly turned to the Soviet Union, which eagerly supplied economic assistance through loans and expanded trade. Now convinced that Castro was a Communist, Eisenhower severed diplomatic relations with Cuba, shortly before leaving office in January, 1961.

The incoming Democratic president, John F. Kennedy, was young, intelligent, charismatic, and ambitious. Surrounding himself with a staff of brilliant advisors, Kennedy and his "action intellectuals" set out to redeem a campaign pledge to achieve American victory in the long on-going Cold War. In his memorable inaugural address, Kennedy proudly proclaimed his willingness to engage in an un-relenting crusade against the aggressive forces of Communism. Thus, it is not surprising that the new president, after being briefed by Eisenhower on the C.I.A. plot to topple Castro, promptly ordered its implementation.

At the time, the plan was highly alluring: C.I.A.-trained Cuban exiles would invade the island at the Bay of Pigs; the masses would cheerfully rise up in rebellion against Castro; and a new Cuban Revolutionary Council, created by the Agency, would assume power. Furthermore, to conceal U.S. involvement, Kennedy initially forbade any American military personnel from directly participating in the assault. Nevertheless, the Bay of Pigs invasion proved to be the biggest fiasco of his presidency. When the 1,453 Cuban refugees hit the beaches on April 17, 1961, they were easily overpowered by Castro's army. No popular uprising ever took place and, by the 19th of April, 114 invaders had been killed (along with four Americans), and nearly 1,200 taken prisoner. On the next day, a humiliated Kennedy met with the press and accepted full responsibility for the disaster.

Privately though, he blasted the C.I.A. for having concocted what he now believed had been a harebrained scheme. Yet, his obsession to get rid of Castro impelled him months later to approve a new C.I.A. project—Operation Mongoose—which eventually came under the supervision of his brother, Attorney General Robert Kennedy. In it, agents interfered with the Cuban economy via sabotage activities, sponsored commando raids on the island from Florida, and conspired with organized crime figures to assassinate Castro. On this last point, it must be added, the president may not have been informed. Still, by 1962 the U.S. had placed a full embargo on Cuban trade and had arranged for that nation's expulsion from the Organization of American States. Lastly, in publicized American military exercises during April of that year in the Caribbean, 40,000 troops rehearsed the liberation of an island's people from an imaginary tyrant named "Ortsac" (Castro spelled backwards).

Aware of all these provocative activities, Castro urgently sought help from the U.S.S.R. During the summer and early autumn of 1962 Nikita Khrushchev, the Soviet premier, obliged his new ally by sending Russian soldiers, military equipment, and arms. Alarmed at the Soviet buildup, Republican Congressional candidates in the upcoming elections demanded decisive U.S. action. In September, Kennedy responded with strong warnings to the U.S.S.R. not to ship any "offensive" weapons that would endanger American security. While Khrushchev gave assurances that all of the weapons were "defensive," he began the construction of eighteen intermediate-range (2,200-mile) and twenty-four medium-range (1,020-mile) missile sites in Cuba. When operational, the nuclear missiles would have a capability of killing 92,000,000 Americans. *(See cover art.)*

Precisely why Khrushchev made such a daring move remains a subject of debate. Historians have offered a variety of motives: to force negotiations for the Soviet takeover of West Berlin; to compel the U.S. to withdraw its missiles in Turkey that were aimed at the U.S.S.R.; and to disprove Communist China's claim that Khrushchev had become too accommodating with the West. More likely, they insist, the Soviet chairman saw a chance for a vastly improved first-strike capability with nuclear weapons only ninety miles from American shores. Finally, in a viewpoint that has gained increasing acceptance (and the reason Khrushchev himself stated in his later memoirs), he acted primarily to discourage a potential U.S. invasion of Cuba.

No controversy, however, surrounds Kennedy's reaction to the news of what Khrushchev had done. On October 16, within hours of being shown photographic evidence of the missile sites obtained from U-2 reconnaissance aircraft, the president created what would later be known as the Executive Committee of the National Security Council (ExComm). Its purpose was to find a solution to the crisis and its membership was comprised of the "action intellectuals" and other trusted advisors—including Vice-President Lyndon Johnson, Secretary of State Dean Rusk, Defense Secretary Robert McNamara, Assistant Defense Secretary Paul Nitze, Chief Counsel Ted Sorensen, National Security Advisor McGeorge Bundy, Chairman of the Joint Chiefs of Staff Maxwell Taylor, U.N. Ambassador Adlai Stevenson, former Secretary of State Dean Acheson, and the president's brother, Attorney General Robert F. Kennedy.

One of the many intense meetings of the ExComm (JFK Library)

Over a grueling and stressful thirteen-day period, the president and ExComm members proposed and debated various American responses and possible Soviet counter-responses. Interestingly, at the first meeting on October 16, an early discussion focused on the significance of the missiles in Cuba. All agreed that, in sheer numbers, their presence did not alter the overall nuclear balance. Indeed, to meet the 170 ICBMs (intercontinental ballistic missiles) in the American arsenal, the U.S.S.R. could then muster only about a dozen; and, in regard to total atomic warheads, the U.S. enjoyed overwhelming superiority with a seventeen-to-one ratio. Nonetheless, it was argued, the Cuban missiles not only threatened America's east coast, but the Kennedy administration as well. In light of Khrushchev's promise not to install any "offensive" weapons on the island, the president, if he did nothing, would appear to be both a weakling and a fool. In short, the missiles had to be removed.

During the first week of ExComm sessions, two distinct groups formed. The "hawks" (led by Taylor, Nitze, and Acheson) favored an immediate "surgical" air strike to destroy the missile sites and/or a full-scale invasion. Critics, though, quickly pointed out the liabilities —an air attack could not wipe out all of the missiles, thousands of Russian soldiers and Cuban civilians would be killed, and the U.S.S.R. might retaliate with an attack on West Berlin or Turkey. Condemning any surprise air strike as a "Pearl Harbor in reverse," Robert Kennedy passionately told the gathering that "my brother is not going to be the Tojo of the 1960s."

Coalescing under the leadership of McNamara, the "doves" (who included Rusk, Sorensen, and Robert Kennedy) proposed a less provocative alternative—a naval blockade or "quarantine" of Cuba that would prevent any further arms shipments. This was a bold and flexible first step, they insisted, since it demonstrated U.S. resolve while leaving the door open for negotiations or military action. Clearly, though, as some scholars have noted, the term "dove" here is somewhat misleading. When, in fact, Soviet expert Charles Bohlen and Stevenson both urged only straightforward, private talks with the Russians to solve the crisis, they were openly ridiculed.

After briefing his cabinet, Congressional leaders, and foreign allies, President Kennedy announced his decision in a nationwide television broadcast. Before a stunned American public, learning of the Cuban situation for the first time, Kennedy engaged in a risky piece of brinkmanship: he declared the naval quarantine; he requested U.N. assistance in settling the dispute; he demanded the immediate dismantling, under U.N. supervision, of the missiles in Cuba; and he warned that any missiles fired at the U.S. from the island would result in an all-out American nuclear attack on the U.S.S.R. As the president spoke, 180 U.S. ships plied Caribbean waters, 550 B-52 planes (carrying nuclear bombs) went airborne, nearly 250,000 troops began to assemble in Florida, and U.S. military forces worldwide went on full alert.

Public opinion polls revealed that 80% of Americans supported the blockade, but that 60% feared that war was imminent. From Moscow, an angry and defiant Khrushchev denounced U.S. actions and accused Kennedy of bringing the world to the edge of a thermonuclear night-mare. As twenty-five Russian ships continued on course to Cuba, the president reduced the original quarantine line from 800 to 500 miles to give the Soviet leader more time to think. Then, on October 24, just as the vessels were approaching the boundary line, they halted. "We're eye-ball to eyeball," observed Rusk, "and I think the other fellow just blinked."

Two days later, Khrushchev sent a long, emotional letter to Kennedy. Appealing to both sanity and "statesmanlike wisdom," the Soviet pre-mier offered a peaceful way out of the crisis—the withdrawal of the missiles in exchange for an American public pledge never to invade Cuba. Events on October 27, however, shattered all optimism and made it the gloomiest day of the ordeal. First, the Soviets shot down a U-2 plane over Cuba, prompting the "hawks" to push harder for military reprisals. Hours later, another U-2 aircraft that had veered off course in northeastern Siberia was pursued by Russian planes until an Ameri-can squadron arrived on the scene. Finally, the FBI reported that Russian diplomats had ordered the destruction of sensitive documents, which was interpreted as a sign of war.

Moreover, on that same day, the White House received a second message from Khrushchev. Perhaps spurred by hardliners in the Kremlin, a more combative Soviet leader now insisted on an additional conces-sion: the disengagement of U.S. missiles in Turkey. Acting on his brother's suggestion, the president ignored this last dispatch and agreed to the terms Khrushchev first offered on October 26. Meanwhile, in a secret move not made public until the appearance of Robert Kennedy's memoirs in 1969, the Attorney General privately promised the Soviets that the missiles in Turkey would be removed. In addition, as Rusk revealed in 1987, if Khrushchev still rejected this deal, President Kennedy had also secretly made arrangements for the United Nations to advocate a "missile swap" in both Cuba and Turkey.

On October 28, however, Khrushchev accepted Kennedy's proposals and people throughout the world breathed a collective sigh of relief. Yet, even while the missiles in Cuba were being dismantled, several festering problems remained. An irate Castro, who had felt slighted during the whole affair, vehemently objected to UN monitoring of the missile removal and to the withdrawal of Soviet IL-28 bombers (an added demand by Kennedy). Finally, on November 20, after some heated bargaining, Khrushchev announced that he would take back the Russian aircraft; and the U.S., in turn, at last terminated its naval blockade. Interestingly, since Castro refused to yield on any UN inspection, Kennedy declined to honor his pledge not to invade Cuba.

At the time, the American people wildly cheered President Kennedy in his "finest hour" and public approval ratings soared to 75%. Similarly, some historians have praised him for his courage and masterful skills in "crisis management." Others, however, have argued that Kennedy foolishly risked a nuclear disaster with his brinkmanship heroics. Far from being in firm control of events, they note, Kennedy narrowly averted war over the two U-2 plane incidents and made decisions during the period while working under false assumptions. There were 42,000 Russians troops in Cuba, for example, not the 10,000 he was told. Most ominously, he did not know that some nuclear weapons there were already operational and that Soviet commanders had authority to use them should the U.S. attack the island.

In fact, on the twenty-fifth anniversary of the crisis, two of Kennedy's closest advisors offered remarkably candid reassessments. With the passage of time, Ted Sorensen had now come to believe that the confrontation between the two superpowers was "unwise, unwarranted, and unnecessary." Robert McNamara, meanwhile, added that the crisis was not effectively managed due to "misinformation, miscalculation, misjudgment, and human fallibility." Hence, in retrospect, it was indeed fortunate that Kennedy and Khrushchev in the end were willing to negotiate a peaceful settlement. In this regard, both men "blinked." For his part, Khrushchev backed down for several reasons: his inability to defend Cuba from invasion; his recognition of Soviet nuclear inferiority; and his fear that some incident might spark World War III—perhaps initiated by Castro, who apparently pressed him to launch a nuclear strike against the U.S. on October 26.

In all, the Cuban missile crisis had significant results. Vowing never again to be placed at a disadvantage, Soviet leaders embarked on a massive nuclear arms buildup until, by decade's end, they had caught up with the United States. In the meantime, American covert operations and assassination plots against Castro continued and U.S.-Cuban relations remained severely strained for years. Among the more positive consequences, Kennedy and Khrushchev agreed to install a new "hot line" teletype link between Washington and Moscow to improve direct communication. Also, as a hopeful first step toward eventual disarmament, both men signed the Limited Test Ban Treaty of 1963, which outlawed atmospheric and underwater nuclear testing.

Finally, having stared down the nuclear abyss and viewing the cataclysmic horrors that awaited mankind, Kennedy now dedicated himself to promoting genuine world peace. Abandoning the inflammatory Cold War rhetoric of his early years, the president soared to eloquence in perhaps the finest speech of his career at American University in June, 1963. Here, he lamented the huge expenditures on weapons systems, appealed for arms control, and called for conciliation and mutual understanding with the U.S.S.R. Indeed, when speaking of the Russian people, Kennedy reminded his countrymen of certain timeless truths:

> "For, in the final analysis, our most basic common link is that we all inhabit this small planet. We all breathe the same air. We all cherish our children's future. And we are all mortal."

Meeting the Communist Threat

Inaugural Address by John F. Kennedy

Although hailed as one of the most eloquent presidential inaugural addresses, Kennedy's speech has also received criticism. Dealing almost exclusively with foreign affairs and using alarmist rhetoric, the young president issued a stern warning to the Communist world. This "Cold Warrior" approach would characterize the Kennedy administration during its first two years. The following selection contains portions of that historic address.

Source: *Public Papers of the Presidents of the United States, John F. Kennedy*, 1961 (Washington, D.C.: U. S. Government Printing Office, 1962), pp. 1-3.

Inaugural Address

January 20, 1961

The world is very different now. For man holds in his mortal hands the power to abolish all forms of human poverty and all forms of human life. And yet the same revolutionary beliefs for which our forebears fought are still at issue around the globe—the belief that the rights of man come not from the generosity of the state but from the hand of God.

We dare not forget today that we are the heirs of that first revolution. Let the word go forth from this time and place, to friend and foe alike, that the torch has been passed to a new generation of Americans—born in this century, tempered by war, disciplined by a hard and bitter peace, proud of our ancient heritage—and unwilling to witness or permit the slow undoing of those human rights to which this nation has always been committed, and to which we are committed today at home and around the world.

Let every nation know, whether it wishes us well or ill, that we shall pay any price, bear any burden, meet any hardship, support any friend, oppose any foe to assure the survival and the success of liberty.

....

In the long history of the world, only a few generations have been granted the role of defending freedom in its hour of maximum danger. I do not shrink from this responsibility —I welcome it. I do not believe that any of us would exchange places with any other people or any other generation. The energy, the faith, the devotion which we bring to this endeavor will light our country and all who serve it—and the glow from that fire can truly light the world.

And so, my fellow Americans: ask not what your country can do for you-ask what you can do for your country.

My fellow citizens of the world: ask not what America will do for you, but what together we can do for the freedom of man.

September 13, 1962 Press Conference

Beginning in the summer of 1962, Nikita Khrushchev and the Soviets increased the shipment of military weapons (including nuclear missiles) to Cuba. In late August, Senator Kenneth B. Keating, a Republican from New York, publicly claimed that the Russians were constructing missile bases on the island. After American U-2 reconnaissance planes failed to detect evidence of this, President Kennedy made two separate announcements in September. The following are excerpts from his second press conference on the subject.

STATEMENT BY PRESIDENT KENNEDY ON CUBA,
September 13, 1962

There has been a great deal of talk on the situation in Cuba in recent days both in the Communist camp and in our own, and I would like to take this opportunity to set the matter in perspective.

....

Ever since communism moved into Cuba in 1958, Soviet technical and military personnel have moved steadily onto the island in increasing numbers at the invitation of the Cuban government. Now that movement has been increased. It is under our most careful surveillance. But I will repeat the conclusion that I reported last week, these new shipments do not constitute a serious threat to any other part of this Hemisphere.

If the United States ever should find it necessary to take military action against Communism in Cuba, all of Castro's Communist-supplied weapons and technicians would not change the result or significantly extend the time required to achieve that result....But let me make this clear once again: If at any time the Communist buildup in Cuba were to endanger or interfere with our security in any way...or become an offensive military base of significant capacity for the Soviet Union, then this country will do whatever must be done to protect its own security and that of its allies.

We shall be alert to, and fully capable of, dealing swiftly with any such development. As President and Commander in Chief I have full authority now to take such action, and I have asked the Congress to authorize me to call up reserve forces should this or any other crisis make it necessary.

....

We shall continue to work with Cuban refugee leaders who are dedicated as we are to that nation's future return to freedom. We shall continue to keep the American people and the Congress fully informed. We shall increase our surveillance of the whole Caribbean area. We shall neither initiate nor permit aggression in this Hemisphere.

With this in mind, while I recognize that rash talk is cheap, particularly on the part of those who did not have the responsibility, I would hope that the future record will show that the only people talking about a war and invasion at this time are the Communist spokesmen in Moscow and Havana, and that the American people, defending as we do so much of the free world, will in this nuclear age, as they have in the past, keep both their nerve and their head.

The Installation of Missiles

The Cuban Missile Crisis

Following his removal from power in 1964, Nikita Khrushchev composed a series of entertaining, if tainted, memoirs of his remarkable life. In the next selection, the former Soviet premier offered his version of the decision to place nuclear missiles in Cuba.

Source: Nikita Khrushchev, Strobe Talbott, trans. and ed., *Khrushchev Remembers: The Last Testament*, Boston: Little, Brown, and Co., 1974, pp. 509-511.

Fidel Castro was our friend, and revolutionary Cuba was threatened by the saber-rattling militarists of the Pentagon. Reactionary circles in the United States treated Cuba as a festering sore on their country's own body.

....

The United States, on the other end, was bent on directly interfering in the internal affairs of Cuba. The Americans wanted to force Cuba away from the path of socialism and make it drag behind American policy, just as it had before the victory of the Cuban revolution, when puppet presidents made it easy for the U.S. to exploit Cuba.

For our part, we wanted Cuba to remain revolutionary and socialist, and we knew Cuba needed help in order to do so. Cuba is a small island in both population and territory. It doesn't have much industry of its own, and its army is equipped with weapons bought from other countries....It was up to us to supply it.

We had no other way of helping them meet the American threat except to install our missiles on the island, so as to confront the aggressive forces of the United States with a dilemma: if you invade Cuba, you'll have to face a nuclear missile attack against your own cities. Our intention was to install the missiles not to wage war against the U.S., but to prevent the U.S. from invading Cuba and thus starting a war. All we wanted was to give the new progressive system created in Cuba by Fidel Castro a chance to work.

....

We stationed our armed forces on Cuban soil for one purpose only: to maintain the independence of the Cuban people and to prevent the invasion by a mercenary expeditionary force which the United States was then preparing to launch. We had no intention of starting a war ourselves. We've always considered war to be against our own interests. We've never thought in terms of any other than defensive war. Anyone with an ounce of sense can see I'm telling the truth. It would have been preposterous for us to unleash a war against the United States from Cuba. Cuba was 11,000 kilometers from the Soviet Union. Our sea and air communications with Cuba were so precarious that an attack against the U.S. was unthinkable.

Russian freighter on its way to Cuba reveals missile components. (National Archives)

General Anatoly I. Gribkov Recalls the Soviet Military Buildup in Cuba (1962), 1992

As part of the Soviet General Staff in 1962, General Anatoly I. Gribkov was among those who helped set up nuclear weapons in Cuba. At a special conference of scholars and original participants thirty years later, Gribkov disclosed that certain missiles were operational and that Russian commanders were permitted to fire them had Americans invaded the island. Here Gribkov provided an in-depth view of the military situation at the time of the crisis.

Source: Gribkov, Anatoly I., quoted in James G. Blight, Bruce J. Allyn, and David A. Welch, *Cuba on the Brink: Castro, The Missile Crisis, and the Soviet Collapse,* New York; Pantheon Books, 1993, pp. 57-62.

What was the force that we would have to train in our country in a very short span of time and transport to the other side of the ocean? This was its composition:

- A medium-range missile division. We saw this unit as a means to prevent aggression; I repeat, as a means to deter aggression. This division was made up of five regiments. Three were R-12 (NATO designation SS-4) regiments, with missiles whose range was 2,500 km (24 launchers with a complement of 1 1/2 missiles for each launcher). Two were R-14 (SS-5) missile regiments (sixteen launchers, also 1 1/2 missiles per launcher). Forty launchers were foreseen in all, together with the appropriate number of missiles (sixty). I would like to add that at the beginning of the crisis—that is, on October 22nd—three R-12 regiments were already in Cuba, and two regiment sites were already laid out in their deployment areas. The third regiment site was under construction. The two R-14 regiments were still en route at sea, and in accordance with the instructions of the Soviet government, returned to the Soviet Union.

- Two air defense missile divisions comprised of twenty-four missile sites: 144 S-75 (NATO designation SA-2) launchers. The Americans are probably familiar with these data, but I can repeat their range (65 km) and altitude (100 m to 30 km).

- Four motorized rifle regiments, reinforced by three tactical nuclear missile batteries—six launchers for *Luna* (NATO designation FROG, or Free Rocket Over Ground) missiles with a 60 km range. We initially considered calling these units brigades, but then we changed our minds and decided to call them regiments that we were going to deploy there to defend the shores and the missile sites, jointly with the Cuban troops.

- The Air Force had a regiment of forty MiG-21 aircraft in Cuba; thirty-three tactical aircraft (Il-28s); and a separate naval squadron of nine Il-28 aircraft. At the onset of the crisis, only six planes had been assembled, and only a few flights had been made.

- Two regiments of tactical cruise missiles were also provided. In each regiment, there were ten launchers: one for training, and nine for combat. There were eighteen combat launchers in all. Range: 150 km. We brought over eighty conventional cruise missiles for these two regiments.

- We also had an Mi-8 transport helicopter regiment, and a transport air squadron with nine already-obsolete Li-2 planes.

- Now the Navy. We planned to deploy two squadrons to Cuba: one squadron of surface ships, comprising two cruisers and two destroyers; and a squadron of submarines, comprising eleven submarines. These two squadrons never went to Cuba. They were scheduled to be sent out later.

- A missile regiment for coastal defense, with the *Sopka* missile, had eight launchers at four sites on the coast. Thirty-two cruise missiles were brought for these eight launchers. The range of the missiles against targets at sea was 80 km. The Americans are familiar with these data; that's why I merely mention them.

- Finally, there was a brigade of twelve missile-launching *(Komar)* patrol boats, with two P-15 missiles each, with a range of 40 km....

....

Before the crisis, we had foreseen bringing in 45,000 men. By the time of the crisis, we had brought in 42,000. Never before in the history of the Soviet Armed Forces and in the history of Russia had we transported so many troops to the other side of the ocean.

....

Allow me to say that, considering all the possible options in the event of an attack against Cuba, the aggressor would have suffered great losses, either in the event of an air attack with a subsequent landing, or in a direct assault. An air attack would not have destroyed all the missiles. Even if the three intermediate-range missile regiments had been destroyed, leaving only the six *Luna* launchers (which were very hard to destroy), they would have been made ready with nuclear weapons, and we are all perfectly aware of the fact that losses would have been tremendous.

....

Allow me to say that the wisdom and common sense of the three leaders—Fidel Castro, Kennedy, and Khrushchev —prevented a catastrophe. But the world was on the brink of a nuclear holocaust.

The Crisis Begins

During its six-minute surveillance flight over Cuba on October 14, 1962, an American U-2 plane took 928 photographs that revealed for the first time the existence of Soviet missile sites under construction. After two more missions the next day and further analysis of the pictures, President Kennedy was finally notified on the morning of October 16. Within hours, he convened an emergency meeting of his principal advisors—later known as the Executive Committee of the National Security Council (ExComm). Over the next thirteen days, the "action intellectuals" would be put to their most severe test. Because Kennedy had planted a secret taping system in the White House and some tapes have been declassified, historians have been treated to a fascinating behind-the-scenes look at the handling of the crisis. The following selection features conversations from the first meeting.

Kennedy and McNamara (JFK Library)

Source: *Foreign Relations of the United States, 1961-1963, Volume II.* (Washington, D.C.: U.S. Government Printing Office, 1996), pp. 31, 33-34, 37, 42-43, 57-58. Transcript of a Meeting at the White House.

Washington, October 16, 1962, 11:50 a.m.

JFK: Secretary Rusk?

Rusk: Yes. (Well?), Mr. President, this is a, of course, a (widely?) serious development. It's one that we, all of us, had not really believed the Soviets could, uh, carry this far....Now, um, I do think we have to set in motion a chain of events that will eliminate this base. I don't think we (can?) sit still. The questioning becomes whether we do it by sudden, unannounced strike of some sort, or we, uh, build up the crisis to the point where the other side has to consider very seriously about giving in, or, or even the Cubans themselves, uh, take some, take some action on this.

....

But I think that, by and large, there are, there are these two broad alternatives: one, the quick strike; the other, to alert our allies *and* Mr. Khrushchev that there is utterly serious crisis in the making here, and that, uh...Mr. Khrushchev may not himself really understand that or believe that at this point. I think we'll be facing a situation that could well lead to general war; that we have an obligation to do what has to be done but do it in a way that gives, uh, everybody a chance to, uh, put the (word unintelligible) down before it gets too hard....

McNamara: Mr. President, there are a number of unknowns in this situation I want to comment upon, and, in relation to them, I would like to outline very briefly some possible military alternatives and ask General Taylor to expand upon them.

But before commenting on either the unknowns or outlining some military alternatives, there are two propositions I would suggest that we ought to accept as, uh, foundations for our further thinking. My first is that if we are to conduct an air strike against these installations, or against any part of Cuba, we must agree now that we will schedule that prior to the time these missile sites become operational. I'm not prepared to say when that will be, but I think it is extremely important that our talk and our discussion be founded on this premise: that any air strike will be planned to take place prior to the time they become operational. Because, if they become operational before the air strike, I do not believe we can state we can knock them out before they can be launched; and if they're launched there is almost certain to be, uh, chaos in part of the east coast or the area, uh, in a radius of six hundred to a thousand miles from Cuba.

Uh, secondly, I, I would submit the proposition that any air strike must be directed not solely against the missile sites, but against the missile sites plus the airfields plus the aircraft which may not be on the airfields but hidden by that time plus all potential nuclear storage sites. Now, this is a fairly extensive air strike. It is not just a strike against the missile sites; and there would be associated with it potential casualties of Cubans, not of U.S. citizens, but potential casualties of Cubans in, at least in the hundreds, more likely in the low thousands, say two or three thousand. It seems to me these two propositions, uh, should underlie our, our discussion.

....

Rusk: Still, about why the Soviets are doing this, um, Mr. McCone suggested some weeks ago that one thing Mr. Khrushchev may have in mind is that, uh, uh, he knows that we have a substantial nuclear superiority, but he also knows that we don't really live under fear of his nuclear weapons to the extent that, uh, he has to live under fear of ours. Also we have nuclear weapons nearby, in Turkey and places like that. Um....

JFK: How many weapons do we have in Turkey?

Taylor?: We have Jupiter missiles...

Bundy?: Yeah. We have how many?

McNamara?: About fifteen, I believe it is....

Rusk: Um, and that Mr. McCone expresses the view that Khrushchev may feel that it's important for us to learn about living under medium-range missiles, and he's doing that to sort of balance that, uh, that political, psychological (plank?). I think also that, uh, Berlin is, uh, very much involved in this. Um, for the first time, I'm beginning really to wonder whether maybe Mr. Khrushchev is entirely rational about Berlin. We've (hardly?) talked about his obsession with it. And I think we have to, uh, keep our eye on that element. But, uh, they may be thinking that they can either bargain Berlin and Cuba against each other, or that they could provoke us into a kind of action in Cuba which would give an umbrella for them to take action with respect to Berlin. In other words like the Suez-Hungary combination. If they could provoke us into taking the first overt action, then the world would be confused and they would have, uh, what they would consider to be justification for making a move somewhere else. But, uh, I must say I don't really see the rationality of, uh, the Soviets pushing it this far unless they grossly misunderstand the importance of Cuba to this country.

....

JFK: Uh, eh, well, this, which....What you're really talking about are two or three different, uh, (tense?) operations. One is the strike just on this, these three bases. One, the second is the broader one that Secretary McNamara was talking about, which is on the airfields and on the SAM (surface-to-air missile) sites and on anything else connected with, uh, missiles.

Third is doing both of those things and also at the same time launching a blockade, which requires really the, uh, the, uh, third and which is a larger step. And then, as I take it, the fourth question is the, uh, degree of consultation....

RFK: We have the fifth one, really, which is the invasion. I would say that, uh, you're dropping bombs all over Cuba if you do the second, uh, air, the airports, knocking out their planes, dropping it on all their missiles. You're covering most of Cuba. You're going to kill an awful lot of people, and, uh, we're going to take an awful lot of heat on it....

....

JFK: I think we ought to, what we ought to do is, uh, after this meeting this afternoon, we ought to meet tonight again at six, consider these various, uh, proposals....I don't think we got much time on these missiles....We're certainly going to do number one; we're going to take out these, uh, missiles. Uh, the questions will be whether, which, what I would describe as number two, which would be a general air strike. That we're not ready to say, but we should be in preparation for it. The third is the, is the, uh, the general invasion. At least we're going to do number one, so it seems to me that we don't have to wait very long. We, we ought to be making *those* preparations.

....

McNamara: Mr. President, could I outline three courses...

JFK?: (Yes?)

McNamara: ...of action we have considered and speak very briefly on each one? The first is what I would call the political course of action, in which we, uh, follow some of the possibilities that Secretary Rusk mentioned this morning by approaching Castro, by approaching Khrushchev, by discussing with our allies....This seemed to me likely to lead to no satisfactory result, and it almost *stops* subsequent military action. Because the danger of starting military action *after* they acquire a nuclear capability is so great I believe we would decide against it, particularly if that nuclear capability included aircraft as well as, uh, uh, missiles, as it well might at that point.

A second course of action...would involve declaration of open surveillance; a statement that we would immediately impose an, uh, a blockade against *offensive* weapons entering Cuba in the future; and an indication that with our open-surveillance reconnaissance, which we would plan to maintain indefinitely for the future, we would be prepared to immediately attack the Soviet Union in the event that Cuba made any offensive move against this country...

....

But the third course of action is any one of these variants of military action directed against Cuba, starting with an air attack against the missiles....And to move from that into the more extensive air attacks against the MiGs, against the airfields, against the potential nuclear storage sites, against the radar installations, against the SAM sites....To move beyond that into an invasion following the air attack means the application of tens of thousands, between ninety and, and, uh, over a hundred and fifty thousand men to the invasion forces. It seems to me almost certain that any one of these forms of direct military action will lead to a Soviet military response of some type some place in the world. It may well be worth the price.

Radio and Television Report to the American People on the Soviet Arms Buildup in Cuba.

October 22, 1962 (Delivered from the President's Office)

Source: *Public Papers of Presidents of the United States, John F. Kennedy, 1962.* (Washington, D.C.: U. S. Government Printing Office, 1963), pp. 806-809.

Good evening, my fellow citizens:

This government, as promised, has maintained the closest surveillance of the Soviet military buildup on the island of Cuba. Within the past week, unmistakable evidence has established the fact that a series of offensive missile sites is now in preparation on that imprisoned island. The purpose of these bases can be none other than to provide a nuclear strike capability against the Western Hemisphere.

....

This urgent transformation of Cuba into an important strategic base—by the presence of these large, long-range, and clearly offensive weapons constitutes an explicit threat to the peace and security of all the Americas....This action also contradicts the repeated assurances of Soviet spokesmen, both publicly and privately delivered, that the arms buildup in Cuba would retain its original defensive character, and that the Soviet Union had no need or desire to station strategic missiles on the territory of any other nation.

....

Our policy has been one of patience and restraint, as befits a peaceful and powerful nation, which leads a worldwide alliance. We have been determined not to be diverted from our central concerns by mere irritants and fanatics. But now further action is required—and it is under way; and these actions may only be the beginning. We will not prematurely or unnecessarily risk the costs of worldwide nuclear war in which even the fruits of victory would be ashes in our mouth—but neither will we shrink from that risk at any time it must be faced.

Acting, therefore, in the defense of our own security and of the entire Western Hemisphere, and under the authority entrusted to me by the Constitution as endorsed by the resolution of the Congress, I have directed that the following *initial* steps be taken immediately:

First: To halt this offensive buildup, a strict quarantine on all offensive military equipment under shipment to Cuba is being initiated. All ships of any kind bound for Cuba from whatever nation or port will, if found to contain cargoes of offensive weapons, be turned back. This quarantine will be extended, if needed, to other types of cargo and carriers.....

Second: I have directed the continued and increased close surveillance of Cuba and its military buildup....Should these offensive military preparations continue, thus increasing the threat to the hemisphere, further action will be justified. I have directed the Armed Forces to prepare for any eventualities; and I trust that in the interest of both the Cuban people and the Soviet technicians at the sites, the hazards to all concerned of continuing this threat will be recognized.

Third: It shall be the policy of this Nation to regard any nuclear missile launched from Cuba against any nation in the Western Hemisphere as an attack by the Soviet Union on the United States, requiring a full retaliatory response upon the Soviet Union.

Fourth: As a necessary military precaution, I have reinforced our base at Guantanamo, evacuated today the dependents of our personnel there, and ordered additional military units to be on a standby alert basis.

Fifth: We are calling tonight for an immediate meeting of the Organ of Consultation under the Organization of American States, to consider this threat to hemispheric security and to invoke articles 6 and 8 of the Rio Treaty in support of all necessary action. The United Nations Charter allows for regional security arrangements—and the nations of this hemisphere decided long ago against the military presence of outside powers. Our other allies around the world have also been alerted.

Sixth: Under the Charter of the United Nations, we are asking tonight that an emergency meeting of the Security Council be convoked without delay to take action against this latest Soviet threat to world peace. Our resolution will call for the prompt dismantling and withdrawal of all offensive weapons in Cuba, under the supervision of U.N. observers, before the quarantine can be lifted.

Seventh and finally: I call upon Chairman Khrushchev to halt and eliminate this clandestine, reckless, and provocative threat to world peace and to stable relations between our two nations. I call upon him further to abandon this course of world domination, and to join in an historic effort to end the perilous arms race and to transform the history of man. He has an opportunity now to move the world back from the abyss of destruction—by returning to his government's own words that it had no need to station missiles outside its own territory, and withdrawing these weapons from Cuba—by refraining from any action which will widen or deepen the present crisis—and then by participating in a search for peaceful and permanent solutions.

....

My fellow citizens: let no one doubt that this is a difficult and dangerous effort on which we have set out. No one can foresee precisely what course it will take or what costs or casualties will be incurred. Many months of sacrifice and self-discipline lie ahead—months in which both our patience and our will will be tested—months in which many threats and denunciations will keep us aware of our dangers. But the greatest danger of all would be to do nothing.

The path we have chosen for the present is full of hazards, as all paths are—but it is the one most consistent with our character and courage as a nation and our commitments around the world. The cost of freedom is always high—but Americans have always paid it. And one path we shall never choose, and that is the path of surrender or submission.

Our goal is not the victory of might, but the vindication of right—not peace at the expense of freedom, but both peace and freedom, here in this hemisphere, and, we hope, around the world. God willing, that goal will be achieved.

Thank you and good night.

Response to the Public Challenge

Kennedy in the Oval Office, 1962 (JFK Library)

President Kennedy's live, televised speech stunned people throughout the world—including Soviet leaders. Indeed, Khrushchev was infuriated at the president's decision to bypass private negotiations in favor of an intimidating public challenge. On October 24, a defiant Khrushchev wrote Kennedy to inform him that the U.S.S.R. would not yield to American demands. Following are excerpts from that letter.

Source: *Foreign Relations of the United States, 1961-1963, Volume II.* (Washington, D.C.: U.S. Government Printing Office, 1996), pp. 185-187.

Letter from Chairman Khrushchev to President Kennedy

Moscow, October 24, 1962.

DEAR MR. PRESIDENT:

...Just imagine, Mr. President, that we had presented you with the conditions of an ultimatum which you have presented us by your action. How would you have reacted to this? I think that you would have been indignant at such a step on our part. And this would have been understandable to us.

In presenting us with these conditions, you, Mr. President, have flung a challenge at us. Who asked you to do this? By what right did you do this? Our ties with the Republic of Cuba, like our relations with other states, regardless of what kind of states they may be, concern only the two countries between which these relations exist....

You, Mr. President, are not declaring a quarantine, but rather are setting forth an ultimatum and threatening that if we do not give in to your demands you will use force. Consider what you are saying! And you want to persuade me to agree to this! What would it mean to agree to these demands? It would mean guiding oneself in one's relations with other countries not by reason, but by submitting to arbitrariness. You are no longer appealing to reason, but wish to intimidate us.

No, Mr. President, I cannot agree to this, and I think that in your own heart you recognize that I am correct. I am convinced that in my place you would act the same way.

....

You wish to compel us to renounce the rights that every sovereign state enjoys, you are trying to legislate in questions of international law, and you are violating the universally accepted norms of that law. And you are doing all this not only out of hatred for the Cuban people and its government, but also because of considerations of the election campaign in the United States. What morality, what law can justify such an approach by the American Government to international affairs? No such morality or law can be found, because the actions of the United States with regard to Cuba constitute outright banditry or, if you like, the folly of degenerate imperialism. Unfortunately, such folly can bring grave suffering to the peoples of all countries, and to no lesser degree to the American people themselves, since the United States has completely lost its former isolation with the advent of modern types of armament.

Therefore, Mr. President, if you coolly weigh the situation which has developed, not giving way to passions, you will understand that the Soviet Union cannot fail to reject the arbitrary demands of the United States. When you confront us with such conditions, try to put yourself in our place and consider how the United States would react to these conditions. I do not doubt that if someone attempted to dictate similar conditions to you—the United States—you would reject such an attempt. And we also say—no.

The Soviet Government considers that the violation of the freedom to use international waters and international air space is an act of aggression which pushes mankind toward the abyss of a world nuclear-missile war. Therefore, the Soviet Government cannot instruct the captains of Soviet vessels bound for Cuba to observe the orders of American naval forces blockading that Island....Naturally, we will not simply be bystanders with regard to piratical acts by American ships on the high seas. We will then be forced on our part to take the measures we consider necessary and adequate in order to protect our rights. We have everything necessary to do so.

Respectfully,
N. Khrushchev

Initial Reactions

American Reaction to the "Quarantine"

News of the placement of nuclear missiles in Cuba, aimed at the United States, set off a wave of indignation across America. In typical fashion despite the horrific dangers involved, the American people rallied behind the president. The selection below is a sampling of American attitudes from a nationwide survey that was conducted by U.S. News and World Report *magazine.*

Source: *U.S. News and World Report*, November 5, 1962, pp. 38-39.

WHAT AMERICANS THINK ABOUT "QUARANTINE" OF CUBA

Overwhelmingly, Americans across the country backed the action of President Kennedy in the first few days after the U. S. imposed a "quarantine" on Communist Cuba. Most felt that the decision was overdue and hoped that it did not come too late.

Staff members of "U. S. News & World Report" talked with hundreds of people to get their reactions to the international crisis. Satisfaction that the U. S. finally had called for a show-down with Russia on the Cuban issue was widespread. Few people voiced outright opposition.

"Right thing at last." Said a plant manager in San Francisco: "We're doing the right thing at last. It will be over quickly. The Russians will back down on war." An attorney in Oakland, Calif., agreed. He said: "We should have gotten even tougher with Russia. We should have told them to get out of Cuba, lock, stock, and barrel, or else—not just argue about it in the United Nations."

A housewife in Little Rock, Ark., said: "We wanted something like this done long before this. And now that it looks like we may get into a war, we're ready to face it."

"It is a necessary evil," said a salesman in Far Hills, N.J. "We will probably have some swap-offs with the Russians as far as our overseas bases are concerned. Each country will play a little game of chess."

A businessman in Montgomery, Ala., complained: "Kennedy should have moved a lot sooner. Even the children around here have known for a year that Castro planned offensive moves."

"Long past due." To a banker in Iowa, the U.S. action was "long past due." He added: "We are not really spiritually ready for a war, but we should have been. We should have been ready two years ago."

Another Iowan, a Des Moines housewife, said: "I've been worried about this for a long time, but I guess we all feel kind of relieved that we finally stood up and told Castro where to get off."

"I just hope this isn't politics," said an industrial consultant in San Francisco. "It's too dangerous a game for that. If we don't have better information than to be surprised in Cuba, where we should have friends, then we aren't ready for war."

And a newspaper editor in Montgomery, Ala., commented. "Kennedy is on the right track this time. I don't know too much about the legal basis of such a search. There may not be any. But this is the right time to go into Cuba and to clean it up and get it over with. I don't think the Russians will do anything about it."

This from a sales executive in Westport, Conn.: "There comes a point when a major power can't push another major power any further. I'm sure Khrushchev isn't surprised at our reaction. But it's so dangerous that I have reservations. I think we should have at least submitted the problem to the United Nations."

In New York City, a Russian-born accountant, now a U.S. citizen, said: "I'm worried. It's a rough situation. I wish we could get together with the Cubans somehow. But I can't criticize the President for what he did."

"I am glad," said a Little Rock editor, "that instead of reacting to a Communist move, we've acted for a change and now we can see how the Communists react to our move. There's no great alarm among the people I've talked to. They seem to be ready."

Said a gas-station attendant in Millbrae, Calif.: "It won't mean war. Did you ever force an issue on a barking dog? If you have, you know this is what happens: he turns tail and runs. The Russians always keep us off balance while they settle themselves into an area. Now we've done it to them. They'll just start trouble elsewhere."

Said a housewife in Jackson, Miss.: "I hate to say anything nice about that awful man in the White House, but I think he's right this time."

A businessman in Tallahassee, Fla., said: "What Kennedy has done is good for the country—the country's spirit and its spine. It puts us back into the American mold. We have had no leadership for years. We took insults and lies from the Russians and a petty puppet like Castro. Now, thank God, we are doing something about it."

A physician in Providence, R.I., said: "The time has passed" for a showdown with Russia. "Even if it means war," he said, "I am in favor of the President's action."

Playing with danger? In Yonkers, N.Y., a banker warned: "We are playing with dangerous stuff. There is no escape for either the smallest soldier or the biggest general if there is a nuclear war."

A law student in Berkeley, Calif.: "We have no right to tell Cuba what to do. President Kennedy admitted that. But we have no choice—right or wrong—we've too much to lose. We can only hope that we've drawn the right card."

A restaurant hostess in Detroit, with three sons of military age, said: "We can't let the Russians go on bluffing and bullying us."

A different view was voiced by a college co-ed from Port Washington, N.Y., who said: "I don't believe in nuclear testing, the arms race or military force. I believe in a different approach. We are as much to blame as the Russians. But I don't know what should be done about it."

No choice, but—." "If we have the correct facts and the situation affects our security, the President had no choice but to take a stand," said a management engineer in Norwalk, Conn. "But I've seen a lot of decisions made incorrectly because of a lack of the correct facts."

A Florida drug salesman commented: "If President Kennedy had acted sooner, it would have been better. Most people, at least in the South, approve of acting firmly when threatened. The next move now is up to the Russians."

"This is the best time for a showdown," said a union official in Washington, D.C. "We have a good case now. The trouble with this country is that we have traded too long and negotiated too long with the Russians."

The mounting tensions of the crisis also produced some desperate and comical actions. Below is a brief excerpt from Time *magazine, November 2, 1962, p. 27.*

Shotguns and Beans. There were some Nervous Nelly reactions in the U. S. The stock market, hardly a symbol of U. S. backbone, dropped sharply next day. In Tampa, sporting-goods stores reported a run on shotguns and rifles. In Dallas, a store reported brisk sales of an emergency ration pack of biscuits, malted-milk tablets, chocolate, pemmican and canned water.

In Los Angeles, a Civil Defense warning that retail stores would be closed for five days in the event of war or a national emergency sent housewives stampeding into the supermarkets. In one, hand-to-hand combat broke out over the last can of pork and beans. Said North Hollywood Grocer Sam Goldstad: "They're nuts. One lady's working four shopping carts at once. Another lady bought twelve packages of detergents. What's she going to do, wash up after the bomb?" Yet for all such transient evidences of panic, the U.S. was solidly behind Kennedy. As he himself had discovered on his election-year forays around the nation, it was the overriding wish of almost all Americans to "do something" about Cuba....

Civil Defense

By the early 1960s, Americans had been going about their daily lives for more than a decade amid the frightening prospect that at any given moment a devastating nuclear war with the U.S.S.R. might erupt. While it would be profoundly disturbing to many people today, government officials at all levels—including President Kennedy—routinely urged citizens to heed Civil Defense alerts, to engage in air-raid drills, and to build fallout shelters in their backyards. The following article appeared in a Washington newspaper during the tensest week of the crisis.

Source: *Evening Star* (Washington, D.C.) October 24, 1962.

"Civil Defense Shelters Being Stocked, Marked,"

Federal Civil Defense officials today stepped up the provisioning and marking of fallout shelter areas in Government buildings. Emergency supplies—water cans, foodstuffs, medical kits and portable sanitation units—were installed in the Interstate Commerce Commission this morning in a basement shelter area.

Luminous, black and yellow "Fallout Shelter" signs and auxiliary arrow-direction signs were to be installed on and inside the building later today.

Federal and District CD officials said the program for stocking and designating all shelter areas in Washington has been accelerated. A total of 813 shelter areas in Government and private structures in the district were selected in a Federally backed survey last winter....

Throughout the Capital area, CD workers told residents who asked about warning signals that the "alert" sound—indicating air raid danger but not within one hour—is a steady, non-pulsating siren tone of 3-to-5 minutes' duration. The more urgent "take cover" signal is a pulsating, rising and falling, siren tone lasting 3-to-5 minutes.

Personal Reminiscences

Resuming Life with Peace of Mind

For Americans who lived through these terrifying days of late October, 1962, the Cuban Missile Crisis left an indelible imprint. In many respects, the reflections below of Fred Marchion mirror those of millions of other citizens. A veteran of World War II, who had served in the Navy, Marchion took advantage of the G.I. Bill and graduated in 1948 from what is now the University of Hartford. One week after receiving his degree, he married Terry McDonald. By 1962, he had become a successful business executive at Stanley Works in New Britain, Connecticut, and the Marchions and their four children had recently purchased a bigger house in nearby West Hartford.

Source: Letter from Fred Marchion to the editor, September 1, 1997.

My generation grew up very distrustful of the U.S.S.R. We always believed that it was a ruthless Communist dictatorship that was bent on conquering the world. Even though Joseph Stalin was our ally during World War II, I felt it was a big mistake to let the Russians march into Berlin in 1945.

After the war, Stalin refused to pull out of the countries he had overrun in Eastern Europe. And his successor, Nikita Khrushchev, was no better. From his shoe-pounding antics at the United Nations to his threat to America— "We will bury you" —he was one Soviet leader who needed to be put in his place.

Thus, when I heard President Kennedy's speech on October 22, 1962, I thought that it was about time that someone was finally standing up to Khrushchev. If Kennedy had not issued his ultimatum, I felt that it would have been a great disaster for the U.S.A. The nuclear missiles in Cuba could have been launched to kill over 100,000,000 Americans!

With regard to the naval blockade, I was not too concerned with our navy's ability to handle the Russian ships. After all, we were able to patrol both the Atlantic and the Pacific during World War II. So, I was confident that the navy could handle the area around Cuba.

After going through that frightening week in late October, it was a great relief to learn that the Russians backed down. At the time, I thought that JFK did a good job in handling the crisis. But, most of all, I was relieved to know that World War III had been averted. My wife Terry and I and the children—Debbie, Mary-Ann, Ed, and Donna—could go on with our lives with peace of mind.

A Turning Point for the Cuban People

A different perspective is provided by two American citizens who were born in Cuba, Juan and Casimira Vazquez. At the time of the Cuban Missile Crisis, Juan had received a law degree from the University of Havana and was an attorney assigned to the criminal branch of the state judicial system in the province of Matanzas. Casimira, meanwhile, had earned two doctorates from the same university and was a high school vice-principal in Colon.

Refusing to live under a communist regime, they courageously resigned from their positions and suffered the confiscation of all their possessions. Along with their daughter, Amalia, they left their homeland and came to the U.S. in 1965. After settling in Connecticut, they went on to establish distinguished careers at the high school and university levels. Here are their personal recollections.

Source: Letter from Juan and Casimira Vazquez to the editor, September 15, 1997.

After the failed expedition of the Bay of Pigs, known in Cuba as *"Playa Giron,"* a tense atmosphere existed. The Cuban people were now convinced that two, rival external forces were at work to determine the fate of our country. The United States, through its covert operations, was determined to destroy the revolutionary government of Fidel Castro; and the Soviet Union was bent on keeping it in power to serve as a Communist base in the Caribbean.

At the time, it could be said that the Cuban people were divided basically into three categories: those who openly backed the revolution; those who less openly were against it; and those who were still not certain of the eventual direction it would take and were, therefore, undecided.

Before the missile crisis, the general public did not know exactly what was going on. But, many people saw caravans of heavy military trucks pulling huge trailers that carried what looked like large torpedoes covered with dark canvases.

Russian truck, rumbling through Havana

These vehicles traveled mostly at night, with their lights off—which caused many accidents!

When the missile crisis developed, the general feeling was that of consternation. The country was at the brink of becoming a battlefield for the two most powerful nations on the planet who were ready to use the deadliest of all weapons. Those were times when most personal problems seemed unimportant in comparison to the prospect of a holocaust.

Fortunately, diplomacy and common sense prevailed and a great human tragedy was averted. Interestingly, some people theorized that the mastermind of the whole episode was the high-ranking Soviet leader, Anastas Mikoyan. He created the crisis, so the theory goes, to extract from the United States a promise never to attack Castro—a move that would preserve a Russian military base only 90 miles from America. Who knows?

The missile crisis was a turning point for the Cuban people. Those who backed Castro, as well as those who opposed him, became more radical than ever. And those who, up to that time, were doubtful of the regime's direction were now convinced of what the future would be.

"We had come to the time of final decisions."

As the president's brother and attorney general, Robert Kennedy was destined to play a major role during the missile crisis. Young, intelligent, and ambitious, Robert at times served as presiding officer at ExComm sessions. Though he seldom spoke and deliberately sat away from the conference table to minimize his presence, Kennedy became "a force for caution and good sense." Before his tragic assassination in 1968, he completed a gripping, if partisan, account of the crisis in Cuba. In the next selection, Kennedy recalls the anxious events of October 24, when Russian ships steaming toward the island were within only a few miles of the American quarantine zone.

Source: Robert F. Kennedy, *Thirteen Days: A Memoir of the Cuban Missile Crisis* (New York: W. W. Norton and Co., 1969), pp. 67-72.

The next morning, Wednesday, the quarantine went into effect, and the reports during the early hours told of the Russian ships coming steadily on toward Cuba. I talked with the President for a few moments before we went in to our regular meeting. He said, "It looks really mean, doesn't it? But then, really there was no other choice. If they get this mean on this one in our part of the world, what will they do on the next?" "I just don't think there was any choice," I said, "and not only that, if you hadn't acted, you would have been impeached." The President thought for a moment and said, "That's what I think —I would have been impeached."

The choice was to have gone in and taken steps which were not necessary or to have acted as we did. At least we now had the support of the whole Western Hemisphere and all our allies around the world.

This Wednesday-morning meeting, along with that of the following Saturday, October 27, seemed the most trying, the most difficult, and the most filled with tension. The Russian ships were proceeding, they were nearing the five-hundred-mile barrier, and we either had to intercept them or announce we were withdrawing. I sat across the table from the President. This was the moment we had prepared for, which we hoped would never come. The danger and concern that we all felt hung like a cloud over us all and particularly over the President.

The U-2s and low-flying planes had returned the previous day with their film, and through the evening it was analyzed—by now in such volume that the film alone was more than twenty-five miles long. The results were presented to us at the meeting. The launching pads, the missiles, the concrete boxes, the nuclear storage bunkers, all the components were there, by now clearly defined and obvious. Comparisons with the pictures of a few days earlier made clear that the work on those sites was proceeding and that within a few days several of the launching pads would be ready for war.

It was now a few minutes after 10:00 o'clock. Secretary McNamara announced that two Russian ships, the *Gagarin* and the *Komiles*, were within a few miles of our quarantine barrier. The interception of both ships would probably be before noon Washington time. Indeed, the expectation was that at least one of the vessels would be stopped and boarded between 10:30 and 11:00 o'clock.

Then came the disturbing Navy report that a Russian submarine had moved into position between the two ships.

It had originally been planned to have a cruiser make the first interception, but, because of the increased danger, it was decided in the past few hours to send in an aircraft carrier supported by helicopters, carrying antisubmarine equipment, hovering overhead. The carrier *Essex* was to signal the submarine by sonar to surface and identify itself. If it refused, said Secretary McNamara, depth charges with a small explosive would be used until the submarine surfaced.

I think these few minutes were the time of gravest concern for the President. Was the world on the brink of a holocaust?

Was it our error? A mistake? Was there something further that should have been done? —Or not done? His hand went up to his face and covered his mouth. He opened and closed his fist. His face seemed drawn, his eyes pained, almost gray. We stared at each other across the table. For a few fleeting seconds, it was almost as though no one else was there and he was no longer the President.

Inexplicably, I thought of when he was ill and almost died; when he lost his child; when we learned that our oldest brother had been killed; of personal times of strain and hurt. The voices droned on, but I didn't seem to hear anything until I heard the President say: "Isn't there some way we can avoid having our first exchange with a Russian submarine—almost anything but that?" "No, there's too much danger to our ships. There is no alternative," said McNamara. "Our commanders have been instructed to avoid hostilities if at all possible, but this is what we must be prepared for, and this is what we must expect."

We had come to the time of final decision. "We must expect that they will close down Berlin—make the final preparations for that," the President said. I felt we were on the edge of a precipice with no way off. This time, the moment was now —not next week—not tomorrow, "so we can have another meeting and decide"; not in eight hours, "so we can send another message to Khrushchev and perhaps he will finally understand."

No, none of that was possible. One thousand miles away in the vast expanse of the Atlantic Ocean, the final decisions were going to be made in the next few minutes. President Kennedy had initiated the course of events, but he no longer had control over them. He would have to wait—we would have to wait. The minutes in the Cabinet Room ticked slowly by. What could we say now—what could we do?

Then it was 10:25—a messenger brought in a note to John

McCone. "Mr. President, we have a preliminary report which seems to indicate that some of the Russian ships have stopped dead in the water."

Stopped dead in the water? Which ships? Are they checking the accuracy of the report? Is it true? I looked at the clock. 10:32. "The report is accurate, Mr. President. Six ships previously on their way to Cuba at the edge of the quarantine line have stopped or have turned back toward the Soviet Union. A representative from the Office of Naval Intelligence is on his way over with the full report." A short time later, the report came that the twenty Russian ships closest to the barrier had stopped and were dead in the water or had turned around.

"So no ships will be stopped or intercepted," said the President. I said we should make sure the Navy knew nothing was to be done, that no ships were to be interfered with. Orders would go out to the Navy immediately. "If the ships have orders to turn around, we want to give them every opportunity to do so. Get in direct touch with the *Essex*, and tell them not to do anything, but give the Russian vessels an opportunity to turn back. We must move quickly because the time is expiring," said the President.

Then we were back to the details. The meeting droned on. But everyone looked like a different person. For a moment the world had stood still, and now it was going around again.

John and Robert Kennedy, outside the Oval Office (JFK Library)

To the Brink...

October 25, JFK Letter to Khrushchev

When the Russian vessels chose to respect the American naval blockade, President Kennedy and his advisors had scored a victory for the time being. From Moscow, however, Khrushchev threatened to order submarines in the area to sink U.S. ships if the quarantine continued. Undaunted, Kennedy maintained a hardline position and wrote to the Soviet premier, placing full responsibility for the entire state of affairs on the Soviets themselves. Here is Kennedy's letter.

Source: *Foreign Relations of the United States, 1961-1963, Volume 11* (Washington, D.C.: U.S. Government Printing Office, 1996), p. 198.

October 25, 1962

Dear Mr. Chairman:

I have received your letter of October 24, and I regret very much that you still do not appear to understand what it is that has moved us in this matter.

The sequence of events is clear. In August there were reports of important shipments of military equipment and technicians from the Soviet Union to Cuba. In early September, I indicated very plainly that the United States would regard any shipment of offensive weapons as presenting the gravest issues. After that time, this government received the most explicit assurance from your government and its representatives, both publicly and privately, that no offensive weapons were being sent to Cuba. If you will review the statement issued by TASS in September, you will see how clearly this assurance was given.

In reliance on these solemn assurances, I urged restraint upon those in this country who were urging action in this matter at that time. And then I learned beyond doubt what you have not denied—namely, that all these public assurances were false and that your military people had set out recently to establish a set of missile bases in Cuba. I ask you to recognize clearly, Mr. Chairman, that it was not I who issued the first challenge in this case, and that in the light of this record these activities in Cuba required the responses I have announced.

I repeat my regret that these events should cause a deterioration in our relations. I hope that your Government will take the necessary action to permit a restoration of the earlier situation.

Sincerely yours,
John F. Kennedy

October 26, Khrushchev Letter to JFK

On October 26, Khrushchev responded to Kennedy in a long, rambling, and emotional letter. In it, the Soviet leader again stated his views that atomic weapons in Cuba were "defensive" in nature and that the American blockade was illegal. Then, in the first major breakthrough of the crisis, he offered the president a deal: the dismantling of the Cuban missiles in exchange for a U.S. pledge never to invade the island. Yet, he warned, the failure to negotiate reasonably might well "doom the world to catastrophe of thermonuclear war." Here are excerpts from that letter.

Source: *ibid.*, pp. 235, 239-241.

Moscow, October 26, 1962, 7 p.m.

....

Dear Mr. President:

....

If assurances were given by the President and the government of the United States that the USA itself would not participate in an attack on Cuba and would restrain others from actions of this sort, if you would recall your fleet, this would immediately change everything. I am not speaking for Fidel Castro, but I think that he and the Government of Cuba, evidently, would declare demobilization and would appeal to the people to get down to peaceful labor. Then, too, the question of armaments would disappear, since, if there is no threat, then armaments are a burden for every people. Then, too, the question of the destruction, not only of the armaments which you call offensive, but of all other armaments as well, would look different.

....

Let us therefore show statesmanlike wisdom. I propose: we, for our part will declare that our ships, bound for Cuba, are not carrying any armaments. You would declare that the United States will not invade Cuba with its forces and will not support any sort of forces which might intend to carry out an invasion of Cuba. Then the necessity for the presence of our military specialists in Cuba would disappear.

Mr. President, I appeal to you to weigh well what the aggressive, piratical actions, which you declared the USA intends to carry out in international waters, would lead to. You yourself know that any sensible man simply cannot agree with this, cannot recognize your right to such actions.

If you did this as the first step towards the unleashing of war, well then, it is evident that nothing else is left to us but to accept this challenge of yours. If, however, you have not lost your self-control and sensibly conceive what this might lead to, then, Mr. President, we and you ought not now to pull on the ends of the rope in which you have tied the knot of war, because the more the two of us pull, the tighter that knot will be tied. And a moment may come when that knot will be tied so tight that even he who tied it will not have the strength to untie it, and then it will be necessary to cut that knot. And what that would mean is not for me to explain to you, because you yourself understand perfectly of what terrible forces our countries dispose.

Consequently, if there is no intention to tighten that knot and thereby to doom the world to the catastrophe of thermo-nuclear war, then let us not only relax the forces pulling on the ends of the rope, let us take measures to untie that knot. We are ready for this.

These thoughts are dictated by a sincere desire to relieve the situation, to remove the threat of war.

Respectfully yours,
/s/ N. Khrushchev

October 27, Khrushchev Letter to JFK

October 27 was the most nerve-racking day of the crisis. Reports of the Soviet shredding of secret documents and the two tension-filled U-2 plane incidents all cast a sense of gloom over any peaceful resolution to the crisis. Khrushchev made an additional demand: the withdrawal of U.S. missiles in Turkey. Following are passages from that letter.

Source: *ibid.*, pp. 257-260.

Moscow, October 27, 1962.

Dear Mr. President,

....

You wish to ensure the security of your country, and this is understandable. But Cuba, too, wants the same thing; all countries want to maintain their security. But how are we, the Soviet Union, our Government, to assess your actions which are expressed in the fact that you have surrounded the Soviet Union with military bases; surrounded our allies with military bases; placed military bases literally around our country; and stationed your missile armaments there? This is no secret. Responsible American personages openly declare that it is so. Your missiles are located in Britain, are located in Italy, and are aimed against us. Your missiles are located in Turkey.

You are disturbed over Cuba. You say that this disturbs you because it is 90 miles by sea from the coast of the United States of America. But Turkey adjoins us; our sentries patrol back and forth and see each other. Do you consider, then, that you have the right to demand security for your own country and the removal of the weapons you call offensive, but do not accord the same right to us? You have placed destructive missile weapons, which you call offensive, in Turkey, literally next to us. How then can recognition of our equal military capacities be reconciled with such unequal relations between our great states? This is irreconcilable.

....

I therefore make this proposal: We are willing to remove from Cuba the means which you regard as offensive. We are willing to carry this out and to make this pledge in the United Nations. Your representatives will make a declaration to the effect that the United States...will remove its analogous means from Turkey. Let us reach agreement as to the period of time needed by you and by us to bring this about. And, after that, persons entrusted by the United Nations Security Council could inspect on the spot the fulfillment of the pledges made....

We, in making this pledge...will make a statement within the framework of the Security Council to the effect that the Soviet Government gives a solemn promise to respect the inviolability of the borders and sovereignty of Turkey, not to interfere in its internal affairs, not to invade Turkey, not to make available our territory as a bridgehead for such an invasion, and that it would also restrain those who contemplate committing aggression against Turkey, either from the territory of the Soviet Union or from the territory of Turkey's other neighboring states.

The United States Government will make a similar statement within the framework of the Security Council regarding Cuba. It will declare that the United States will respect the inviolability of Cuba's borders and its sovereignty, will pledge not to interfere in its internal affairs, not to invade Cuba itself or make its territory available as a bridgehead for such an invasion, and will also restrain those who might contemplate committing aggression against Cuba, either from the territory of the United States or from the territory of Cuba's other neighboring states.

....

These are my proposals, Mr. President.

Respectfully yours,
N. Khrushchev

Settlement

October 27, Message to Chairman Khrushchev Calling for Removal of Soviet Missiles from Cuba.

Anxious to reach a diplomatic settlement before the crisis spun out of control, Kennedy quickly responded. Acting on advice that was pushed most vigorously from his brother, the president supported the basic terms of Khrushchev's first "offer" of October 26 and ignored the second. Privately, Robert Kennedy assured the Soviets that American missiles in Turkey would be removed within four or five months. Here are excerpts from President Kennedy's reply.

Source: *Public Papers of the Presidents of the United States, John F. Kennedy, 1962* (Washington, D.C.: U.S. Government Printing Office, 1963), pp. 813-814.

October 27, 1962

Dear Mr. Chairman:

I have read your letter of October 26th with great care and welcomed the statement of your desire to seek a prompt solution to the problem. The first thing that needs to be done, however, is for work to cease on offensive missile bases in Cuba and for all weapons systems in Cuba capable of offensive use to be rendered inoperable, under effective United Nations arrangements.

Assuming this is done promptly, I have given my representatives in New York instructions that will permit them to work out this weekend—in cooperation with the Acting Secretary General and your representative—an arrangement for a permanent solution to the Cuban problem along the lines suggested in your letter of October 26th. As I read your letter, the key elements of your proposals—which seem generally acceptable as I understand them—are as follows:

1. You would agree to remove these weapons systems from Cuba under appropriate United Nations observation and supervision; and undertake, with suitable safeguards, to halt the further introduction of such weapons systems into Cuba.

2. We, on our part, would agree—upon the establishment of adequate arrangements through the United Nations to ensure the carrying out and continuation of these commitments— (a) to remove promptly the quarantine measures now in effect and (b) to give assurances against an invasion of Cuba. I am confident that other nations of the Western Hemisphere would be prepared to do likewise.

If you will give your representative similar instructions, there is no reason why we should not be able to complete these arrangements and announce them to the world within a couple of days...

John F. Kennedy

October 28, JFK Response to Khrushchev Broadcast

Shortly after receiving Khrushchev's message, President Kennedy corresponded with the Soviet premier to implement the final agreements as rapidly as possible. Although nagging problems lingered, the dangerously explosive crisis had been successfully defused. In addition, Kennedy directed attention to a topic upon which both men had recently agreed was of utmost importance to all mankind—nuclear disarmament.

Source: *ibid.*, pp. 814-815.

October 28, 1962

Dear Mr. Chairman:

I am replying at once to your broadcast message of October twenty-eight, even though the official text has not yet reached me, because of the great importance I attach to moving forward promptly to the settlement of the Cuban crisis. I think that you and I, with our heavy responsibilities for the maintenance of peace, were aware that developments were approaching a point where events could have become unmanageable. So I welcome this message and consider it an important contribution to peace.

...I consider my letter to you of October twenty-seventh and your reply of today as firm undertakings on the part of both our governments which would be promptly carried out....

....

I agree with you that we must devote urgent attention to the problem of disarmament, as it relates to the whole world and also to critical areas. Perhaps now, as we step back from danger, we can together make real progress in this vital field. I think we should give priority to questions relating to the proliferation of nuclear weapons, on earth and in outer space, and to the great effort for a nuclear test ban. But we should also work hard to see if wider measures of disarmament can

60

be agreed and put into operation at an early date. The United States Government will be prepared to discuss these questions urgently, and in a constructive spirit, at Geneva or elsewhere.

John F. Kennedy

Kennedy, translator, and Khrushchev, in 1961

October 28, Message from Chairman Khrushchev to President Kennedy

Many ExComm officials fully anticipated a Soviet rejection of Kennedy's proposals and discussions again centered around American military measures. Then, on October 28, a message from Nikita Khrushchev, first broadcast over Moscow radio, brought sighs of relief around the globe. In it, he expressed satisfaction with Kennedy's response. Portions of that message follow.

Source: *Foreign Relations of the United States, 1961-1963, Volume 11, op, cit,*. pp. 279-283.

Moscow, October 28, 1962

Dear Mr. President:

I have received your message of October 27, I express my satisfaction and thank you for the sense of proportion you have displayed and for realization of responsibility which now devolves on you for the preservation of the peace of the world.

....

I regard with respect and trust the statement you made in your message of October 27, 1962, that there would be no attack, no invasion of Cuba, and not only on the part of the United States, but also on the part of other nations of the Western Hemisphere, as you said in your same message. Then the motives which induced us to render assistance of such a kind to Cuba disappear.

It is for this reason that we instructed our officers—these means as I had already informed you earlier are in the hands of the Soviet officers—to take appropriate measures to discontinue construction of the aforementioned facilities, to dismantle them, and to return them to the Soviet Union. As I had informed you in the letter of October 27, we are prepared to reach agreement to enable United Nations Representatives to verify the dismantling of these means.

Thus in view of the assurances you have given and our instructions on dismantling, there is every condition for eliminating the present conflict.

....

Respectfully yours,
N. Khrushchev

UNCLASSIFIED

~~CONFIDENTIAL~~

November 21, 1962

MESSAGE FOR CHAIRMAN KHRUSHCHEV

Dear Mr. Chairman:

I have been glad to get your letter of November 20, which arrived in good time yesterday. As you will have seen, I was able to announce the lifting of our quarantine promptly at my press conference, on the basis of your welcome assurance that the IL-28 bombers will be removed within a month.

I am now instructing our negotiators in New York to move ahead promptly with proposals for a solution of the remaining elements in the Cuban problem. I do not wish to confuse the discussion by trying to state our present position in detail in this message, but I do want you to know that I continue to believe that it is important to settle this matter promptly and on reasonable terms, so that we may move on to other issues. I regret that you have been unable to persuade Mr. Castro to accept a suitable form of inspection or verification in Cuba, and that in consequence we must continue to rely upon our own means of information. But, as I said yesterday, there need be no fear of any invasion of Cuba while matters take their present favorable course.

John F. Kennedy letter to Nikita Khrushchev, November 21, 1962

The Quest for Peace

Commencement Address at American University June 10, 1963

At American University on June 10, 1963, John F. Kennedy delivered what is regarded by many to have been the greatest speech of his presidency. Having narrowly averted the worst calamity in human history, the president urgently called for peace, a re-evaluation of American perceptions of the U.S.S.R., and nuclear disarmament.

Khrushchev, who deemed it "the best speech of any American president since Roosevelt," enthusiastically permitted its broadcast behind the Iron Curtain. While Kennedy at times continued to use Cold War language, perhaps to avoid seeming "soft" on Communism, the "Cold Warrior" of the early years had placed himself on the path to world statesmanship.

Source: *Public Papers of the Presidents of the United States, John F. Kennedy, 1963, op. cit.*, pp. 460-462, 464.

....

I have, therefore, chosen this time and this place to discuss a topic on which ignorance too often abounds and the truth is too rarely perceived—yet it is the most important topic on earth: world peace.

What kind of peace do I mean? What kind of peace do we seek? Not a Pax Americana enforced on the world by American weapons of war. Not the peace of the grave or the security of the slave. I am talking about genuine peace, the kind of peace that makes life on earth worth living, the kind that enables men and nations to grow and to hope and to build a better life for their children—not merely peace for Americans but peace for all men and women—not merely peace in our time but peace for all time.

....

No government or social system is so evil that its people must be considered as lacking in virtue. As Americans, we find communism profoundly repugnant as a negation of personal freedom and dignity. But we can still hail the Russian people for their many achievements—in science and space, in economic and industrial growth, in culture and in acts of courage.

....

Today, should total war ever break out again—no matter how—our two countries would become the primary targets. It is an ironic but accurate fact that the two strongest powers are the two in the most danger of devastation. All we have built, all we have worked for, would be destroyed in the first 24 hours. And even in the Cold War, which brings burdens and dangers to so many countries, including this Nation's closest allies—our two countries bear the heaviest burdens. For we are both devoting massive sums of money to weapons that could be better devoted to combating ignorance, poverty, and disease. We are both caught up in a vicious and dangerous cycle in which suspicion on one side breeds suspicion on the other, and new weapons beget counterweapons.

....

So, let us not be blind to our differences—but let us also direct attention to our common interests and to the means by which those differences can be resolved. And if we cannot end now our differences, at least we can help make the world safe for diversity. For, in the final analysis, our most basic common link is that we all inhabit this small planet.

We all breathe the same air. We all cherish our children's future. And we are all mortal.

Third: Let us reexamine our attitude toward the Cold War, remembering that we are not engaged in a debate, seeking to pile up debating points. We are not here distributing blame or pointing the finger of judgment. We must deal with the world as it is, and not as it might have been had the history of the last 18 years been different.

....We must conduct our affairs in such a way that it becomes in the Communists' interest to agree on a genuine peace. Above all, while defending our own vital interests, nuclear powers must avert those confrontations which bring an adversary to a choice of either a humiliating retreat or a nuclear war. To adopt that kind of course in the nuclear age would be evidence only of the bankruptcy of our policy—or of a collective death-wish for the world.

....

The United States, as the world knows, will never start a war. We do not want a war. We do not expect a war. This generation of Americans has already had enough—more than enough—of war and hate and oppression. We shall be prepared if others wish it. We shall be alert to try to stop it. But we shall also do our part to build a world of peace where the weak are safe and the strong are just. We are not helpless before that task or hopeless of its success. Confident and unafraid, we labor on—not toward a strategy of annihilation but toward a strategy of peace.

Suggested Further Reading

Blight, James G. *Cuba on the Brink*, New York: Pantheon Books, 1993.

————— *The Shattered Crystal Ball: Fear and Learning in the Cuban Missile Crisis.* Savage, Maryland: Rowman and Littlefield Publishers, Inc., 1990.

————— *On the Brink: Americans and Soviets Re-examine the Cuban Missile Crisis.* New York: Hill and Wang, 1989.

Chang, Lawrence and Kornbluh, Peter, eds. *The Cuban Missile Crisis, 1962.* New York: The New Press, 1992.

Garthoff, Raymond L. *Reflections on the Cuban Missile Crisis.* Washington, D.C.: The Brookings Institution, 1989.

Giglio, James N. *The Presidency of John F. Kennedy.* Lawrence: The University Press of Kansas, 1991.

May, Ernest and Zelikow, Philip D., eds. *The Kennedy Tapes.* Cambridge: The Belknap Press of Harvard University Press, 1997.

Nathan, James. *The Cuban Missile Crisis Revisited.* New York: St. Martin's Press, 1992.

Paterson, Thomas G. *Contesting Castro: The United States and the Triumph of the Cuban Revolution.* New York: Oxford University Press, 1994.

Thompson, Robert Smith. *The Missiles of October: The Declassified Story of John F. Kennedy and the Cuban Missile Crisis.* New York: Simon and Schuster, 1992.

About the Editor

Karl E. Valois has served as chairman of the Social Studies Department at St. Joseph High School in Trumbull, Connecticut and has taught history at the University of Connecticut. He was awarded a fellowship at Yale University and earned a Ph.D. at the University of Connecticut. Dr. Valois has appeared on radio and television, published more than two dozen articles and has helped to edit two books on world history. He is also the editor of *The Korean War: Limits of American Power*, which was published by Discovery Enterprises, Ltd. as part of the *Perspectives on History Series.*